SCIENTIFIC AMERICAN

MORE SIMPLE SCIENCE FAIR PROJECTS

Grades 3-5

SCIENTIFIC AMERICAN

MORE SIMPLE SCIENCE FAIR PROJECTS

Grades 3-5

by Salvatore Tocci

Illustrated by Bob Wiacek

CHELSEA CLUBHOUSE

An Imprint of Chelsea House Publishers

ACKNOWLEDGMENT

Putting together this book presented some interesting challenges and unexpected developments. I owe a special note of thanks and gratitude to Kate Nunn, whose editorial guidance was pivotal in the completion of this project.

Scientific American: More Simple Science Fair Projects

Chelsea Clubhouse
An imprint of Chelsea House Publishers
132 West 31st Street
New York NY 10001

Library of Congress Cataloging-in-Publication Data
Tocci, Salvatore.
  Scientific American : more simple science fair projects, grades 3-5 / by Salvatore Tocci ; illustrated by Bob Wiacek.
     p. cm.
   ISBN 0-7910-9055-8
  1. Science projects—Juvenile literature. I. Title: More simple science fair projects, grades 3-5. II. Wiacek, Bob, ill. III. Scientific American, inc. IV. Title.
   Q182.3.T635 2006
   507'.8–dc22   2005057097

Edited by Kate Nunn
Cover design by Andy Davies
Interior design by Gilda Hannah
Interior illustrations by Bob Wiacek

Printed in the United States of America

Bang PKG 10 9 8 7 6 5 4

This book is printed on acid-free paper.

CONTENTS

Science writer **Salvatore Tocci** was a high school biology and chemistry teacher for almost 30 years. Now an accomplished author of science-fact books for readers of all ages, his published work includes a high school chemistry textbook, a series of biographies of famous scientists, and two series for young readers on science experiments and chemical elements. He also travels throughout the country to present workshops at national science conventions.

RESOURCES FOR SCIENCE FAIR EXPERIMENTS

Supplies. All of the materials required for the experiments in this book can be found at home or in "houseware supplies" stores and "hardware" stores.

Information and further ideas. It is recommended that readers visit one or more of the following World Wide Web sites for more information on the science involved in this book's experiments, as well as for ideas for other experiments in the same areas of science. If you do not have a computer with an Internet hookup at home, try your school or local library.

http://www.ipl.org/div/kidspace/projectguide/
http://www.sciserv.org/isef/
http://energyquest.ca.gov/projects/index.html
http://www.ars.usda.gov/is/kids/fair/ideasframe.htm
http://kids.gov/k_science.htm
http://canadaonline.about.com/cs/sciencefairideas/
http://www.physics.uwo.ca/sfair/sflinks.htm
http://www.cdli.ca/sciencefairs/
http://www.scifair.org
http://homeworkspot.com/sciencefair/
http://school.discovery.com/sciencefaircentral/scifairstudio/ideas.html
http://www.all-science-fair-projects.com/category0.html

HAVE FUN WITH YOUR SCIENCE FAIR PROJECT

*Y*ou can learn science by reading about it in a book, magazine, or newspaper. However, the best way to learn science is by doing experiments. Not only is doing science experiments more fun, it is also the only way to learn how scientists work. You will find 36 science experiments in this book. Everything you need to do these experiments can be found in your home or at a local supermarket or hardware store.

Every experiment in this book must be done *with the help of an adult*. Both you and the adult should start by reading the *Background Information, Necessary Materials,* and *Procedure* that appear at the start of each experiment. These sections will give you a clear idea of what the experiment is about, the materials you will need to do it,

and the steps you must follow. In some experiments, the *Procedure* will point out that you need the adult to perform a certain step. For example, the *Procedure* may require the use of a sharp knife or hot stove. The adult should perform these steps. However, remember that you must have an adult supervise *all* your work in *every* experiment.

Another safety step is to wear something to protect your eyes while you are doing an experiment. Some of the chemicals used in certain experiments can irritate your eyes if they accidentally splash on your face. If you don't have them handy, you can buy safety goggles in a hardware store.

Before you do any of the experiments in this book, you should get a notebook to write down the results you get and observations

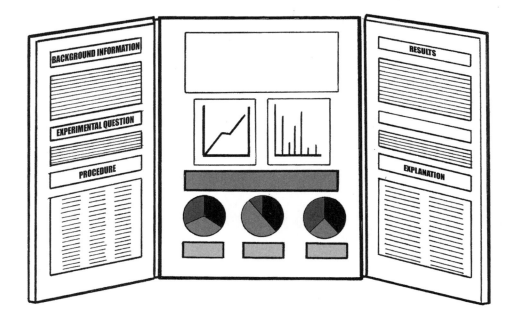

you make. This should be your "lab notebook," where you only keep information that deals with your experiments. Try to keep it as organized as possible so that you can easily locate the information if you need it later.

Think of each experiment as the starting point for learning something about science. For example, you may do the experiment under the heading *Solar Energy*. This experiment shows you how to build a device that will use sunlight to cook vegetables. After you finish this experiment, you can search the Internet. Look for devices that you can build that use sunlight to cook other foods, such as hot dogs. Like any good scientist, you should be creative. For example, can you design and build your own solar cooker?

If you wish, you can use an experiment as a project for your school's science fair. The more information you present in your project, the more interesting it will be. Use an experiment in this book as your starting point. You can then expand the experiment by testing other items. For example, you might do the experiment called "How Do

Antacids Work?" You can then test different antacid tablets to see which works best.

Tips for Your Tabletop Display

Students usually present their science fair projects in the form of a three-sided display. All of the important information from the project is shown on this display. The left hand side of the display can include some background information about your experiment. Place the experimental question you investigated underneath this information. Then include the procedure you followed.

Place the title, your name, and grade at the top of the center of the display. Include all the results you collected. You may simply display the results as you wrote them down in your notebook. However, try to make the display more appealing by including colorful charts and tables of your results.

Showing Your Data

You can include any photographs or drawings that illustrate your procedure on the center panel. You may want to use a graph to display your data. There are many types of graphs, but two that you may find useful are bar graphs and line graphs. For example, a bar chart would help to show the three different sizes of popped kernels of corn in the first experiment in this book, *Solids, Liquids, and Gases*. For the Secondary Experiment in *Solids, Liquids, and Gases*, you could make a line graph by plotting the time values and the temperature values along the X- and Y- axes.

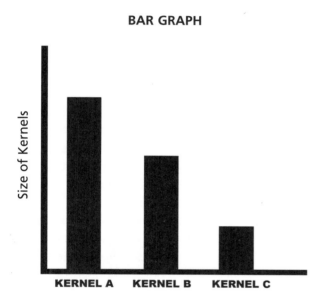

BAR GRAPH

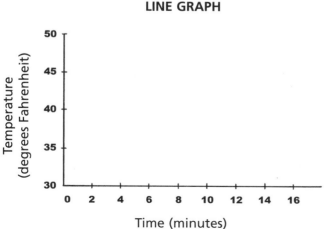

LINE GRAPH

Explaining Your Results

The right hand side of the display usually includes the results of your experiment as you wrote them down in your notebook. Place your explanation underneath the results. Your display will be more impressive if you include information that you discovered on your own. For example, search the Internet for additional information to include in the background information or explanation. Your display will also be more impressive if you show the setup that you used in your experiment. The equipment is usually displayed on the tabletop beside the three-sided display.

You can also check your school library and the Internet for additional information on how to present your project at a science fair.

Show Time!

When you present your display, you need to walk the audience carefully through your experiment. Move from your left panel, to the center, and then to the right. Start by telling your audience the question you asked and taking them through your procedure. Then talk about your data. Explain it fully to them by adding details of your recordings in your lab book. Finally, what conclusion did you come to after doing your experiment? No matter how you present your project, make sure to impress your audience with what you learned and how much fun you had while learning it!

WHAT IS MATTER?

BACKGROUND INFORMATION

Everything in the universe is made of matter. Scientists define matter as anything that has mass and takes up space. For example, this book is matter. The cover and pages are the mass, or "stuff" that make up the book and take up space. In some cases, matter is invisible. An example of invisible matter is the air. The air is made of gases such as oxygen and carbon dioxide. Although these gases have mass and take up space, you cannot see them.

Gases are one of the three types of matter. The other two types of matter are solids and liquids. Solids, liquids, and gases are all made up of tiny building blocks, or particles. However, the way these particles are arranged is different in each type of matter. The particles in a solid are very close to each other and do not move. The particles in a liquid are farther apart and can move past each other. The particles in a gas are much farther apart from each other and move very quickly. **(SEE ILLUSTRATION.)**

One type of matter can be changed into another type of matter. For example, the following experiment involves changing a liquid into a gas. When this happens, the particles move farther apart and make something that you probably like to eat, especially at the movies.

Experimental Question
Why does popcorn pop?

Necessary Materials
- Adult helper
- Measuring cup
- Popping corn
- Container with airtight lid
- Tablespoon
- Oven
- Cookie sheet
- Hot-air popper
- Paper towels

Procedure
1. Place ½ cup of popping corn in a container. Sprinkle with one tablespoon of water. Cover the container and allow it to sit overnight. Gently shake the container every few hours (except when you're asleep).
2. Preheat the oven to 200 degrees. Spread ½ cup of popping corn on a cookie sheet. Bake for two hours. Allow the popping corn to cool.
3. Use the hot-air popper to pop the corn that soaked in water overnight. Spread the popcorn on a paper towel. Label the towel "soaked kernels."
4. Repeat step 3 for the kernels that were baked in the oven. Label the paper towel "baked kernels."

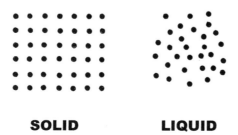

SOLID   LIQUID   GAS

5. Repeat step 3 for regular kernels taken straight from the package. Label the paper towel "regular kernels."
6. Compare the appearance of the three types of popcorn.

Results and Explanation

The kernels that were soaked in water overnight pop the best, followed by the kernels taken from the package. The kernels that were baked in the oven pop the least.

Each kernel contains a tiny amount of moisture, or particles of water. Water is a liquid. The hot-air popper produces heat that changes this water into a gas. Most people call this gas steam. Scientists call it vapor. As the liquid changes into a vapor, the water particles spread out. This causes the kernel to explode, or pop.

The more moisture there is, the more the popcorn kernels will pop. Soaked kernels contain the most moisture. Baked kernels have the least moisture in them. More water vapor is made in kernels that have more moisture. Therefore, the soaked kernels pop the best.

SECONDARY EXPERIMENT

Experimental Question

What happens to the temperature when you change a solid to a liquid?

Necessary Materials

- Adult helper
- Towel
- Ice cubes
- Hammer
- Drinking glass
- Thermometer
- Lamp with incandescent bulb (optional)
- Clock

Procedure

1. Wrap the towel around several ice cubes.
2. Ask the adult to use the hammer to crush the ice.
3. Place the crushed ice inside the glass and cover with water.
4. Place the thermometer inside the glass.
5. Set the glass in direct sunlight or under a lamp.
6. Every minute, use the thermometer to stir the ice water. Stir gently so that you do not break the thermometer.
7. Every two minutes, write down the temperature.
8. Keep taking the temperature every two minutes until all the ice has melted.
9. Take five more temperature readings after all the ice has melted.

Results and Explanation

The temperature does not go up until all the ice is melted. The heat from the sun or lamp first melts the ice. This heat causes the water particles in the ice (solid) to move farther apart from each other to change into water (liquid). When all the ice has melted, the heat raises the temperature of the water.

HOW HOT IS IT?

BACKGROUND INFORMATION

Many people think that heat and temperature are the same, but they are not. Heat is a type of energy. Scientists define energy as the ability to do work. Temperature is a measurement of energy. Temperature tells you how hot or how cold something is.

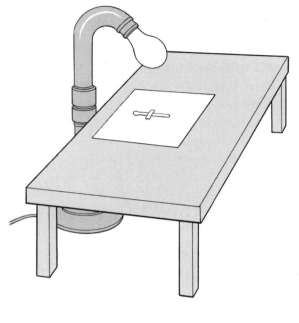

Experimental Question

Do all light bulbs give off the same amount of heat?

Necessary Materials

- Gooseneck lamp
- Table
- Incandescent light bulbs with different wattages, such as 25, 50, and 75 watts
- Sheet of white paper
- Tape
- Thermometer
- Tape measure or yard stick
- Watch or clock with second hand
- Compact fluorescent light bulbs, such as 7 watts and 23 watts

   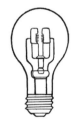

Fluorescent Bulb   **Incandescent Bulb**

Procedure

1. Place the gooseneck lamp near the edge of the table.
2. Screw the lowest wattage incandescent light bulb into the lamp.
3. Plug the lamp into a wall socket. Do not turn on the lamp.
4. Place the white paper on the table close to the lamp.
5. Tape the thermometer to the center of the paper.
6. Measure the distance between the thermometer and the light bulb.
7. Check the thermometer and write down the temperature.
8. Make sure the lamp is pointing directly at the thermometer.
9. Turn on the lamp.
10. Check the thermometer every minute and write down the temperature.
11. Continue to write down the temperature until it no longer rises.
12. Turn off the lamp, unplug it from the wall socket, and allow it to cool for 30 minutes.
13. Replace the light bulb with one that has a higher wattage.
14. Make sure that the distance between the thermometer and the light bulb is the

same as it was in step 6. Also make sure that the temperature on the thermometer is about the same as it was in step 7.

15. Repeat steps 8–14 for each bulb, including at least two compact fluorescent bulbs.

Results and Explanation

The higher the wattage of each bulb, the higher the temperature rises. If you look closely at an incandescent light bulb, you will notice a tiny wire called a filament. As electricity flows through this tiny wire, it gets hot and glows. This glowing produces the light given off by the bulb. The higher the wattage, the hotter the filament gets. Therefore, higher wattage bulbs give off more heat and more light.

Fluorescent light bulbs do not increase the temperature nearly as much as incandescent light bulbs. A fluorescent light bulb works differently than an incandescent bulb. If you look closely at a fluorescent bulb, you will notice that the inside is coated with a white substance. If you could see inside the bulb, you would not see any thin wire. Instead, a fluorescent bulb is filled with a special gas. As electricity passes through the bulb, this gas causes the white coating to give off light. Therefore, a 23-watt fluorescent light bulb gives off much less heat than a 25-watt incandescent light bulb.

SECONDARY EXPERIMENT

Experimental Question

Is plastic or metal the better insulating material?

Necessary Materials

- Goose-neck lamp with 100 watt bulb
- Table
- Tape
- Thermometer
- Sheet of white paper
- Plastic spoon
- Tape measure or yard stick
- Watch or clock with a second hand
- Aluminum foil

Procedure

1. Set up the lamp, paper, and thermometer as you did in the main experiment.
2. Cover the bulb of the thermometer with the plastic spoon.
3. Measure the distance between the thermometer and the light bulb.
4. Check the thermometer and write down the temperature.
5. Make sure the lamp is pointing directly at the thermometer.

6. Turn on the lamp.
7. Check the thermometer every minute and write down the temperature.
8. Continue to write down the temperature until it no longer rises.
9. Turn off the lamp and allow the thermometer to cool.
10. Repeat steps 2–9 with the aluminum foil. Fold the aluminum foil so that it has the same thickness as the plastic spoon. Also make sure that the distance between the thermometer and light bulb is the same in both tests.

Results and Explanation

The temperature increases faster with the aluminum foil than it does with the plastic spoon. The passage of heat through a material, such as metal or plastic, is called conduction. Metals are better conductors than plastics.

Insulators reduce the conduction of heat. For example, the insulation in the walls of a house prevents warm air from moving out in winter. In summer, the insulation prevents warm air from moving into the house. Plastics are better insulators than metals.

HOW CAN YOU FEEL COOLER?

BACKGROUND INFORMATION

Both light and heat are types of energy. One type of energy can be changed into a different type of energy. For example, when you turn on a lamp, electrical energy is changed into light energy. The reason you feel hot on a summer day is because light energy from the sun is changed into heat energy. Find out how you can feel cooler in summer by carrying out the following experiment.

Experimental Question
Why is it a good idea to wear white clothes in summer?

Necessary Materials
- Scissors
- Tape
- Colored construction paper (white, green, brown, and black)
- Thermometer

Procedure
1. Use the scissors and tape to make a small envelope from the white construction paper, which will cover the bulb of the thermometer.
2. Place the covered thermometer in direct sunlight but protected from any wind. You can carry out this experiment any day of the year by using a gooseneck lamp to substitute for sunlight.
3. Record the temperature on the thermometer. Then record the temperature after 5, 10, and 20 minutes.

4. Repeat steps 1–3, this time using a different colored sheet of construction paper. Be sure to let the thermometer to cool each time.

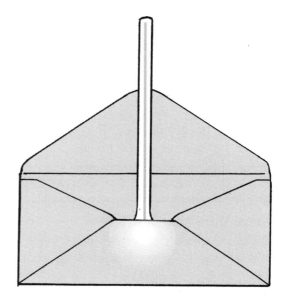

Results and Explanation
The temperature rises the most when the bulb is covered with the black paper. The temperature rises the least when the bulb is covered with the white paper. The green and brown papers cause a temperature increase somewhere between the black and white papers.

Dark colors absorb light. This light is changed into heat, which causes the temperature to rise. In contrast, white does not absorb light. Instead, white reflects light. Therefore, the light is not changed into heat. For this reason, you should wear dark colors in cool weather to feel warmer and white on hot days to feel cooler.

SECONDARY EXPERIMENT

Experimental Question
How can sunlight blow up a balloon?

Necessary Materials
- Black and white spray paint
- Two empty plastic soda bottles
- Two small balloons
- Gooseneck lamp (optional)

Procedure
1. Ask an adult to spray paint one bottle white and the other bottle black. Allow the paint to dry thoroughly.
2. Stretch the balloons so that they can inflate more easily.
3. Place the open end of a balloon over the mouth of each bottle. Be sure that the balloon and bottle form an airtight seal.
4. Place both bottles in direct sunlight. If it is cloudy, place the bottles under a lamp.
5. Observe what happens to the balloons.
6. Touch the bottles to see how each one feels.

Results and Explanation
The balloon on the black bottle should inflate. The balloon on the white bottle should remain limp. The black paint absorbs the light, which changes into heat. This heat warms the air inside the bottle. As air warms, it spreads out, or expands. As the air expands in the black bottle, the air flows into the balloon. As a result, the balloon starts to inflate. Because the white paint reflects the light, the air inside the bottle does not get warm. Therefore, the air inside the white bottle does not expand and inflate the balloon.

HOW CAN SUNLIGHT BE USEFUL?

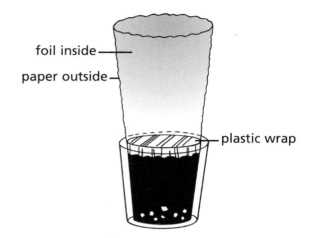

foil inside

paper outside

plastic wrap

BACKGROUND INFORMATION

The Earth is about 93 million miles from the sun. Yet sunlight takes only about 8.5 minutes to travel that distance. Once sunlight reaches Earth, this light is used for several purposes. Plants use sunlight to make food and grow. Animals use sunlight to keep warm. People use sunlight to heat water for their homes. The following experiment shows another way that sunlight can be useful.

Experimental Question

How can you use sunlight to cook?

Necessary Materials

- Black poster paint and brush
- Two Styrofoam™ cups
- Small pieces of vegetables that you can eat raw, such as carrots and cauliflower
- Plastic wrap
- Rubber band
- Scissors
- Aluminum foil
- Sheet of construction paper, 8½ by 11 inches.
- Transparent tape
- Shoe box filled with sand or dirt

Procedure

1. Paint the inside of one of the cups with the black poster paint. Allow the paint to dry thoroughly.
2. Place several small vegetable pieces inside the cup.
3. Cover the cup with plastic wrap. Use the rubber band to hold the plastic wrap in place.

4. Cut a piece of aluminum foil so that it is the same size as the construction paper.
5. Tape the aluminum foil to the construction paper. Make sure that the shiny side is up, and avoid getting any wrinkles in the foil.
6. Wrap the aluminum foil around the cup so that the foil faces inward. Use the tape to hold the foil in place.
7. Place the foil-covered cup inside the second cup. The second cup will provide more insulation to prevent heat from escaping.
8. Bury the cups in the sand or dirt so that the aluminum foil is exposed. Bury the

cups at an angle so that they point toward the sun.

9. Keep the cups pointed at the sun by moving the shoe box.

10. After 10 minutes, remove the cups and take off the plastic wrap. Check the vegetables to see if they are cooked. If not, put them back inside the cup, replace the plastic wrap, and test them again later.

Results and Explanation

Depending on how sunny it is, the vegetables should cook very quickly. The black paint inside the cup absorbs the sunlight that is reflected by the aluminum foil through the plastic wrap and into the cup. This light energy is changed into heat energy. The plastic wrap acts as an insulator, preventing the heat from escaping. Trapped inside the cup, the heat cooks the vegetables.

SECONDARY EXPERIMENT

Experimental Question

Why is it hot in summer and cold in winter?

Necessary Materials

- Flashlight
- Transparent tape
- Thermometer
- Sheet of black paper
- Magnifying lens

Procedure

Do this part of the experiment in a dark room.

1. Turn on the flashlight and point it directly downward at the floor. Notice the size of the area that the light covers.

2. Turn the flashlight so that it shines on the floor at an angle. Compare the size of the area that the light covers to the area that was covered when you held the flashlight pointing directly downward.

Do this part of the experiment in full sunlight.

3. Use the tape to fasten the thermometer to the paper.

4. Record the temperature.

5. Place the thermometer on a flat surface near a window or on the ground outdoors.

6. Hold the magnifying lens to focus the sunlight so that it strikes the thermometer at an angle.

7. Record how high the temperature gets.

8. Place the thermometer in the shade so that it cools.

9. Again, place the thermometer and paper near a window or outdoors.

10. Hold the magnifying lens this time so that the sunlight is focused directly downward on the thermometer.

11. Record how high the temperature gets.

Results and Explanation

Light covers a smaller area when it shines directly from overhead rather than from an angle. The temperature gets higher when you focus sunlight directly downward on the thermometer rather than at an angle.

Earth is actually closer to the sun in January than in June. Then why does the temperature in the Northern Hemisphere get hot in June and cold in January? The answer has to do with the way sunlight strikes Earth during these months. Earth is tilted on its axis. In summer, the Northern Hemisphere is tilted toward the sun. The sun is higher in the sky, causing the sun's rays to shine directly onto Earth. This focuses the rays into a smaller area, making it warmer.

In winter, the Northern Hemisphere is tilt-ed away from the sun. The sun is lower in the sky, causing the sun's rays to shine on Earth at an angle. This causes the rays to spread out over a wider area, making it cooler.

DIRECT SUN RAYS IN SUMMER

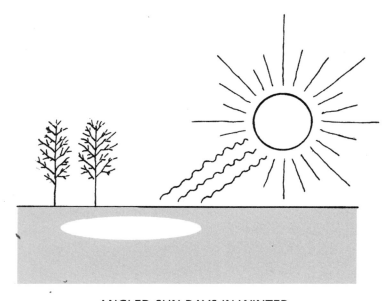

ANGLED SUN RAYS IN WINTER

WHERE DID THE SUGAR GO?

BACKGROUND INFORMATION

Have you ever gargled with salt water to make a sore throat feel better? Making the salt water is easy—just add some salt to a glass of water and stir. Stirring causes the salt to dissolve in the water. Dissolving means that the salt breaks into smaller and smaller pieces so that you can no longer see them in the water. Salt dissolved in water is an example of a solution. Soda pop is another example. Soda pop is made by dissolving several substances in water. One of these substances is sugar.

Experimental Question

How much sugar can you dissolve in a glass of water?

Necessary Materials

- Measuring cup
- Tall, clear drinking glass
- ¼ teaspoon measuring spoon
- Sugar

Procedure

1. Pour 1 cup of cold water into the glass.
2. Add ¼ teaspoon of sugar and stir until all the sugar is dissolved.
3. Add another ¼ teaspoon of sugar and stir again, until all the sugar is dissolved.
4. Continue adding sugar, ¼ teaspoon at a time, until no more sugar dissolves.
5. Record how many ¼ teaspoons of sugar you dissolved in the cup of cold water.
6. Rinse out the glass.
7. Repeat steps 1–6, this time using 1 cup of warm water.
8. Repeat steps 1–6, this time using 1 cup of hot water.

Results and Explanation

More sugar dissolves in warm water than in cold water, and more sugar dissolves in hot water than in warm water. The warmer you make the water, the more sugar you can dissolve.

Both sugar and water are made of very tiny substances called molecules. Warming the water causes the water molecules to move faster. The faster the water molecules move, the more sugar molecules they break apart, or dissolve.

SECONDARY EXPERIMENT

Experimental Question

How much salt can you dissolve in a glass of water?

Necessary Materials

- Measuring cup
- Tall, clear drinking glass
- ¼ teaspoon measuring spoon
- Salt

Procedure

1. Pour 1 cup of cold water into the glass.
2. Add ¼ teaspoon of salt and stir until all the salt is dissolved.
3. Add another ¼ teaspoon of salt and stir again, until all the salt is dissolved.
4. Continue adding salt, ¼ teaspoon at a time, until no more salt dissolves.
5. Record how many ¼ teaspoons of salt you

dissolved in the cup of cold water.
6. Rinse out the glass.
7. Repeat steps 1–6, this time using 1 cup of warm water.
8. Repeat steps 1–6, this time using 1 cup of hot water.

Results and Explanation

About the same amount of salt dissolves in cold, warm, and hot water. These results show that dissolving a substance does not always happen in the same way. Dissolving is a complicated process that involves more than just the temperature of the water. The process also depends on the chemical nature of the substance that is being dissolved. Sugar and salt are two different types of chemical substances. The dissolving of sugar is affected by temperature, whereas the dissolving of salt is not.

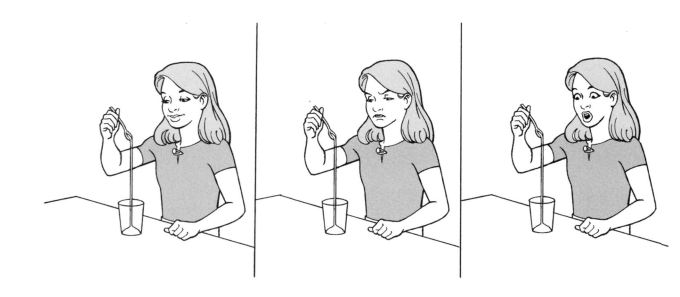

WHERE DID THE WATER GO?

BACKGROUND INFORMATION

All living things are made of tiny building blocks called cells. Some living things, such as bacteria, are made of only one cell. Most living things, however, are made of many cells. For example, the human body is made of trillions of cells. All these cells need certain things to survive. One thing that all cells need is water.

All cells are surrounded by a thin layer called a membrane. Water is constantly moving across this membrane. Sometimes water moves across the membrane from inside the cell to the outside. At other times, water moves across the membrane from outside the cell to the inside. The movement of water across a membrane is called osmosis. The following experiment will show you why water moves in a certain direction.

Experimental Question

Which way does water move by osmosis?

Necessary Materials

- Adult helper
- Knife
- Potato
- Ruler
- Two small glasses
- Salt
- Teaspoon
- Clock

Procedure

1. Ask the adult to cut two strips from the potato. Each strip should be about the size of a French fry and about ½ inch thick.
2. Fill each glass half full with water. Add two teaspoons of salt to one glass. Stir until all the salt dissolves in the water.
3. Place one potato strip in the salt water. Place the other potato strip in the plain water. Allow both strips to soak for about 60 minutes.
4. Remove the potato strips. Describe how each strip feels.

Results and Explanation

The potato strip soaked in salt water feels limp. The potato strip soaked in plain water feels firm.

Water moves by osmosis whenever there is a difference in concentration. Concentration refers to how much of something there is in a certain space. To understand what concentra-

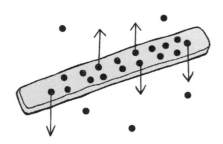

SALT WATER

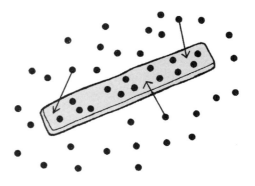

PLAIN WATER

tion means, picture your classroom. Imagine that you are alone in the room. Now imagine the same room filled with all your classmates. When the room is filled, it has a higher concentration of classmates.

When soaked in salt water, a potato strip has a higher concentration of water. Water always moves by osmosis from a higher concentration to a lower concentration. Therefore, water moves from the potato into the salt water. The potato feels limp because it loses water.

When soaked in plain water, a potato strip has a lower concentration of water. In this case, water moves from the plain water into the potato. The potato feels firm because it gains water.

SECONDARY EXPERIMENT

Experimental Question
What happens to an egg soaked in water?

Necessary Materials
- Egg
- Drinking glass
- Vinegar
- 12-inch piece of string
- Ruler

Procedure
1. Place the egg in the glass and cover it with vinegar.
2. Allow the egg to soak in the vinegar for 2–3 days.
3. Carefully remove the egg and very gently rinse it with water. Describe how the egg feels.

4. Measure the size of the egg by gently wrapping the string around its middle. Hold your finger on the spot where the end of the string meets the rest of the string. Stretch the string along the ruler to measure the size of the egg.
5. Rinse the glass with water. Carefully place the egg in the glass. Fill the glass with water so that it covers the egg. Allow the egg to soak in the water for 3–4 days.
6. Carefully remove the egg and repeat Step 4. How does the size of the egg compare to its original size?

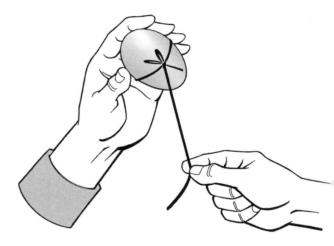

Results and Explanation
The egg gets larger. Vinegar dissolves the shell covering the egg. Removing the shell exposes the membrane that surrounds the egg. When the egg is soaked in water, the water concentration is higher outside the egg. Water moves by osmosis across the membrane and into the egg. As the egg gains water, it gets larger. Experiment to see what happens to the size of the egg if you soak it in salt water rather than in plain water.

WHAT IS A CATALYST?

BACKGROUND INFORMATION

Chemical changes are constantly occurring around you. Examples of chemical changes include the rusting of an iron nail and the burning of gasoline in a car's engine. Both rusting and burning are examples of chemical reactions. A chemical reaction is a process in which one or more substances change into one or more new substances. For example, gasoline burned in a car's engine is changed into new substances, including carbon dioxide gas.

Burning gasoline in an engine is an example of a chemical reaction that occurs very quickly. In contrast, the rusting of an iron nail is an example of a chemical reaction that takes place very slowly. Sometimes a chemical reaction that is slow must be speeded up. A substance called a catalyst is often used to speed up a chemical reaction.

Experimental Question

How can you show that a catalyst speeds up a chemical reaction?

Necessary Materials

- Measuring cup
- Hydrogen peroxide
- Small, clear drinking glass
- Teaspoon
- Sugar
- Piece of fresh liver or potato
- Knife

Procedure

1. Pour 2 ounces of hydrogen peroxide into the glass.

2. Look closely at the hydrogen peroxide and describe what you see.
3. Add a teaspoon of sugar to the hydrogen peroxide.
4. Look closely and describe what you see.
5. Add a small piece of liver or potato to the hydrogen peroxide.
6. Look closely and describe what you see.

7. Rinse out the glass.
8. Pour 2 ounces of fresh hydrogen peroxide into the glass.
9. Ask an adult to use a knife to chop up a small piece of liver or potato.
10. Add the chopped liver or potato to the hydrogen peroxide.
11. Look closely and describe what you see.

Results and Explanation

Hydrogen peroxide is a clear liquid that looks like water. Nothing happens when you add sugar. However, bubbles appear when you add liver or potato. Even more bubbles appear when you chop up the liver or potato.

A chemical reaction is taking place inside a bottle of hydrogen peroxide. The hydrogen peroxide is very slowly being changed into new substances. Adding sugar does not make this chemical reaction happen any faster. However, adding liver or potato makes this chemical reaction happen much faster. The bubbles that you see are bubbles of oxygen gas. Oxygen is one of the new substances made from hydrogen peroxide. The liver and potato contain a catalyst that speeds up the chemical reaction. Chopping the liver or potato exposes more catalysts. This is why the chemical reaction happens even faster when you add the chopped liver or potato.

SECONDARY EXPERIMENT

Experimental Question
What can gas bubbles do?

Necessary Materials
- Measuring cup
- Vinegar
- Plastic bag with zipper-lock
- Paper napkin
- Tablespoon
- Baking soda
- String
- Scissors
- Kitchen sink or bathtub

Procedure
1. Add ½ cup of cold water and ½ cup of vinegar to the plastic bag.
2. Seal the bag and make sure that it does not leak.
3. Place 2 tablespoons of baking soda in the middle of the paper napkin.
4. Fold the paper napkin into a pouch to hold the baking soda.
5. Tie the opening of the pouch with a piece of string.
6. Open the plastic bag.
7. Drop the paper napkin into the plastic bag and zip it closed.
8. Place the bag in the sink or bathtub. Watch what happens.

Results and Explanation
A chemical reaction takes place inside the bag. This time you do not need to add a catalyst. The vinegar and baking soda quickly react to produce new substances. One of these new substances is carbon dioxide gas. These are the bubbles that pop open the bag.

You can experiment by trying different sized plastic bags, by mixing the vinegar with warm water, or by using only vinegar. See which method produces the most bubbles that pop open the plastic bag. By the way, a similar chemical reaction takes place when a cake is baked. The heat from the oven causes a chemical reaction. The baking soda added to the recipe produces carbon dioxide bubbles that make the cake rise.

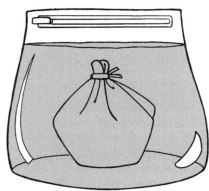

HOW CAN YOU CHANGE THE COLOR?

BACKGROUND INFORMATION

There are millions of different chemicals. Scientists form chemicals into groups, just as they do with animals and plants. The members of each group have something in common. For example, scientists group many chemicals as either acids or bases. The chemicals that are acids have a sour or tart taste. Acids are usually liquids or gases. Both vinegar and the liquid inside a car battery are examples of acids. Bases have a slippery feeling. Bases are usually solids or liquids. For example, drain cleaner is a base commonly called lye, which can be bought as either a solid or a liquid.

Although acids and bases are different, they are similar in some ways. Some acids and bases can cause serious skin burns. For example, anyone whose skin comes in contact with either battery acid or drain cleaner should thoroughly rinse the area with running water. However, the acids and bases you will use in the following experiment do not cause skin burns.

Experimental Question

How can you tell the difference between an acid and a base?

Necessary Materials
- Adult helper
- Knife
- Red cabbage
- Large pot
- Stove
- Cheesecloth or coffee filter
- Bowl
- Rubber band

- Clear drinking glass
- Household products such as lemon juice, vinegar, ammonia, seltzer water, and clear liquid soap

Procedure
1. Ask an adult to chop the cabbage into small pieces.
2. Add 2 cups of the cabbage to a large pot.
3. Cover the cabbage with water and boil for 10 minutes.
4. Allow the liquid to cool to room temperature.
5. Cover the bowl with a piece of cheesecloth or coffee filter. Use a rubber band to secure the cheesecloth or filter to the bowl.
6. Slowly pour the contents of the pot through the piece of cheesecloth or coffee filter. **(See illustration, next page)**
7. Collect the purplish liquid in the bowl.
8. Pour 2 ounces of the purplish liquid into a clear glass.
9. Slowly pour lemon juice into the glass until you see the color change.
10. Rinse out the glass.
11. Repeat steps 6–8, this time using a different household product, such as vinegar, ammonia, seltzer water, or clear liquid soap.
12. Save the purplish liquid in the container if you plan to do the Secondary Experiment.

Results and Explanation

Adding lemon juice, vinegar, or seltzer water turns the cabbage solution a reddish color. Adding ammonia or clear liquid soap turns the cabbage solution a greenish or yellowish color.

The cabbage solution contains a colored substance called a pigment. This pigment

changes color, depending on whether it is in an acid or a base. Lemon juice, vinegar, and seltzer water are acids. The pigment from the cabbage turns red in acids. Ammonia and liquid soap are bases. The pigment from the cabbage turns greenish-yellow in bases.

SECONDARY EXPERIMENT

Experimental Question
How do antacids work?

Necessary Materials
- Measuring cup
- Purplish liquid from red cabbage
- Clear drinking glass
- Antacid tablets
- Teaspoon

Procedure
1. Pour 2 ounces of the purplish liquid into a clear glass.
2. Slowly pour lemon juice into the glass until you see a reddish color.
3. Add an antacid tablet and stir with the teaspoon until the tablet dissolves.
4. If the color does not change, add another antacid tablet and stir. Continue adding antacid tablets until you see the color change.

Results and Explanation
Adding the antacid changes the color of the cabbage solution from red to greenish-yellow. Antacids tablets are taken when a person has an upset stomach. This feeling is caused by too much acid being produced by the stomach. An antacid tablet contains a base. A base reduces the effect of an acid. Scientists say that a base neutralizes an acid. Therefore, an antacid can get rid of an upset stomach by neutralizing the excess acid.

HOW CAN YOU KEEP THE LIGHTS ON?

BACKGROUND INFORMATION

Everything in the universe is made of atoms. Atoms are so small that until recently no one had ever seen one. An atom can be seen only with a very powerful microscope. As small as it is, an atom consists of even smaller bits called particles. One of these particles is called an electron. Electrons usually zoom around the center of an atom. However, electrons can move or flow from one atom to another.

Electrons can be made to flow from one atom to the next atom in a wire. A steady flow of electrons through a wire produces a current of electricity that we call electricity. As long as the electrons keep flowing, electricity is flowing through the wire. If the wire is cut, then electricity will stop flowing. However, you can get the electricity flowing again. All you have to do is rejoin the cut wires. Or you can connect the two cut pieces with something that will allow electrons to flow through it. Anything that allows electrons to flow through it is called a conductor. Anything that does not allow electrons to flow through it is called an insulator.

Experimental Question

How can you tell if something is a conductor or an insulator?

Necessary Materials

- Flashlight
- Electrical tape
- Scissors or wire cutter
- Ruler
- Copper wire
- Large paper clip
- Various household items such as string, rubber band, key, toothpick, and hair pin

Procedure

1. Remove the batteries and bulb from the flashlight.
2. Use electrical tape to join the two batteries, keeping them in the same position as you found them in the flashlight.
3. Cut two 6-inch pieces of copper wire.
4. Tape an end of one copper wire to the negative end (flat end) of the batteries.
5. Tape an end of the other copper wire to the positive end (metal cap) of the batteries.
6. Touch the free end of one wire to the metal base of the bulb.
7. Touch the free end of the other copper wire to the metal ring at the bottom of the bulb.

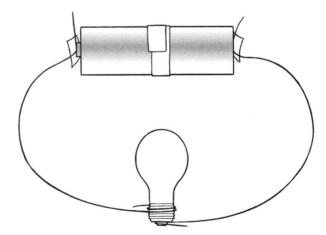

8. Watch what happens to the bulb.
9. Cut one of the copper wires.
10. Straighten a paper clip.
11. Touch one end of the paper clip to one free end of the cut wire.

12. Touch the other end of the paper clip to the other free end of the cut wire.

13. Watch what happens to the bulb.
14. Repeat steps 10–13 each time using a different item to connect the cut wire—a piece of string, a rubber band, a key, a toothpick, or any other small object you have at home. Keep track of which objects allow the bulb to light up.

Results and Explanations

The bulb lights up when a conductor is used to join the cut wires. Metals, such as paper clips and keys, are good conductors. These conductors allow electricity to flow from one cut wire to the other cut wire.

The bulb does not light up when an insulator is used to join the cut wires. String, rubber, and wood are insulators. These insulators do not allow electricity to flow from one cut wire to the other, so the bulb will not light up.

SECONDARY EXPERIMENT

Experimental Question

What is static electricity?

Necessary Materials

- Small fluorescent light bulb
- Plastic comb
- Wool sock
- Helper with a clock or watch with a second hand

Procedure

1. Take the materials into a closet and close the door.
2. Wait until your eyes adjust to the darkness.
3. Rub the comb back and forth with the sock for at least two minutes. Ask your helper to tell you when two minutes have passed.
4. Touch the comb to the middle of the light bulb.
5. Look quickly and closely inside the bulb.

Results and Explanation

When you hold the comb against the bulb, it should glow for a short time. If the bulb does not glow, rub the comb longer with the wool sock.

As you rub the comb, electrons move from the sock to the comb. These electrons collect on the comb. When you hold the comb against the bulb, the electrons jump from the comb to the bulb. These electrons produce tiny sparks, or a glow inside the bulb. In this case, electrons do not keep flowing. Rather, electrons jump from one object to another.

When electrons jump like this, they produce static electricity. Static electricity is what gives you a small shock when you touch a metal doorknob on a cold day. Static electricity also produces lightning.

HOW DO BATTERIES WORK?

BACKGROUND INFORMATION

Batteries come in many different sizes and shapes. However, all batteries have something in common. They produce electricity. They also contain chemical substances that allow electricity to flow through them.

In the previous experiment, you learned that everything in the universe is made of atoms. In turn, atoms are made of even smaller bits, or particles called electrons. Electricity is the flow of electrons from one atom to another atom. Therefore batteries must somehow cause electrons to flow from one atom to another. You can make a simple battery to see how it produces electricity.

Experimental Question

How can you make a battery from a lemon?

Necessary Materials

• Scissors or wire cutters
• Ruler
• Copper wire
• Two large paper clips
• Two pennies
• Two large lemons
• Adult helper
• Knife
• Several light-emitting diodes, LEDs (found at electronic supply stores such as Radio Shack®)

Procedure

1. Cut three pieces of copper wire, each about 6 inches long
2. Wrap the ends of two wires around the two large paper clips.
3. Wrap the end of one of these wires around one of the pennies.

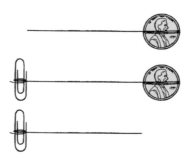

4. Wrap the end of the third wire around the other penny.
5. Gently squeeze and roll the lemons on a table or counter top.
6. Ask an adult to make two small cuts through the skins of each lemon, each about 1 inch apart.
7. Insert the penny attached to the paper clip into one of the slits in a lemon.
8. Insert the paper clip at the other end of the wire into a slit in the other lemon.
9. Insert the second penny into the open slit in one lemon.
10. Insert the second paper clip into the open slit in the other lemon.
11. Make sure that the pennies and paper clips are all in the juicy part of the lemons.
12. Touch the free ends of the two copper wires to the light-emitting diode. 13. Watch what happens to the diode. A diode conducts electricity in only one direction. If the flow is reversed, the diode will burn

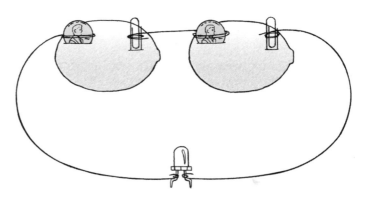

out. You may go through a few diodes before you find out how to connect the copper wires to the diode.

Results and Explanation

The diode lights up as electricity flows through it. Electrons travel through the lemons and the wires to light the diode. The paper clip and the penny are made of two different metals. The paper clip is made partly of iron atoms. The penny is made partly of copper atoms. Electrons leave the iron atoms in the paper clips and travel through the wires to the copper atoms in the pennies. As long as the lemon juice keeps the electrons flowing through the wires, the diode will stay lit.

SECONDARY EXPERIMENT

Experimental Question

How can you make a potato clock?

Necessary Materials
- Two large galvanized nails
- Two potatoes
- Marking pen
- Scissors or wire cutter
- Ruler
- Copper wire
- Three alligator clips (found at electronic supply stores such as Radio Shack®)
- LED clock that operates with one AAA battery.

Procedure
1. Label the potatoes with a marking pen as 1 and 2.
2. Insert one nail into each potato near one end.
3. Cut two pieces of copper wire, each about 6 inches long.
4. Insert the end of a copper wire into each

potato. Place the copper wire at the other end of each potato, as far from the nails as possible.
5. Remove the battery from the clock. Locate the positive (+) and negative (-) terminals on the clock. The positive terminal is usually a metal strip, and the negative terminal is usually a spring.
6. Use an alligator clip to connect the nail in potato 1 to the copper wire in potato 2.
7. Use a second alligator clip to connect the nail in potato 2 to the negative terminal (spring) in the clock.
8. Attach the third alligator clip to the copper wire in potato 1. Then touch the free end of this alligator clip to the positive terminal (metal strip) in the clock.
9. Watch what happens to the clock.

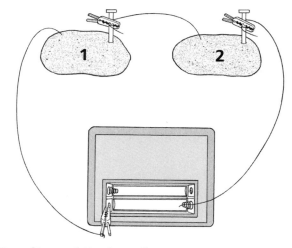

Results and Explanation

The clock starts running when the last connection is made. Galvanized nails are covered with a metal called zinc. The zinc protects the nail from rusting. Electrons flow from the zinc to the copper. Like the lemons, the potatoes help to keep the electrons flowing through the wires. You can experiment to see which other items will keep the clock running. Do sweet potatoes work as well as potatoes? In place of potatoes, try oranges, limes, apples, and pears.

WHY DO THINGS SLOW DOWN?

BACKGROUND INFORMATION

Walking down a steep hill can be tricky. You have to take each step very carefully so that you do not slip. Fortunately, there is a force that is helping you. A force is a push or pull that can either start an object moving or stop it from moving.

The force that helps you walk down a steep hill is friction. Friction is a force that acts against motion. Friction is one of the forces that slow down a ball rolling along the ground. Friction does not affect all objects in the same way, as you can check out by doing the following experiment.

Experimental Question

Which material overcomes friction best?

Necessary Materials

- Scissors
- Aluminum foil
- Sandpaper
- Felt
- Waxed paper
- Ruler
- Wooden board, about 3 feet long and 1 foot wide
- Quarter
- Clock or watch with second hand
- Magnifying lens
- Baby oil or cooking oil

Procedure

1. Cut strips of aluminum foil, sandpaper, felt, and waxed paper. Each strip should be as long as the wooden board and about 3 inches wide.
2. Tape the strips next to each other so that they run vertically along the board.

3. Lean one end of the board against a box to make a ramp.
4. Hold a quarter flat against one of the strips at the top of the ramp.
5. Release the quarter.
6. Time how long it takes for the quarter to reach the bottom of the ramp.
7. Repeat steps 4–6, placing the quarter on a different strip each time.
8. Use the magnifying glass to look closely at each material you taped to the board.
9. Describe what you see.
10. Lightly coat one surface of the quarter with the oil.
11. Hold the oiled surface of the quarter against the aluminum foil at the top of the ramp.
12. Count how long it takes for the quarter to reach the bottom of the ramp.
13. Repeat steps 10–11, holding the quarter against the waxed paper.

Results and Explanation

The quarter slides down the aluminum and waxed paper the fastest. The quarter slides down the felt and sandpaper the slowest. When you look at the felt and sandpaper closely with a magnifying glass, you see that their surfaces are rough. There is more friction when the quarter slides across a rough surface. Because there is more friction, the quarter moves slower.

The quarter slides faster when you cover its surface with a slippery substance such as oil. The oil reduces friction. Because there is less friction, the object will move faster. For example, a skater can quickly glide across the ice because both the ice and skates are smooth and slippery.

SECONDARY EXPERIMENT

Experimental Question
Why do basketball players wear sneakers?

Necessary Materials
• Pencil
• Large plastic or paper cup
• Sneaker
• Table
• Pennies
• Leather-soled shoe, same size as sneaker

Procedure
1. Use the pencil to punch two holes through the paper cup. The holes should be near the top and opposite each other.
2. Undo the laces from a sneaker, except for the pair of holes nearest the toe.
3. Insert a lace through each hole in the cup and tie a knot so that the cup can hang freely from the laces.
4. Place the sneaker on the table so that the cup hangs over the edge.
5. Place one penny at a time in the paper cup until the sneaker falls off the table.

6. Write down how many pennies you added to the cup.
7. Repeat steps 2–6 with the leather-soled shoe.
8. Write down how many pennies you added to the cup before the shoe fell from the table.

Results and Explanation
More pennies must be added to the cup to get the sneaker to fall from the table. The surface of the shoe is smooth and slippery. The surface of the sneaker is bumpy. Therefore, there is more friction when the sneaker moves across the table compared to the shoe moving across the table. Because there is more friction, the sneaker needs more force to move. More pennies in the cup creates a greater force pulling on the sneaker. You can check to see how friction works by testing how a sneaker and shoe move across other types of surfaces, such as wood and marble, too.

WHY DO OBJECTS FALL?

BACKGROUND INFORMATION

An astronaut standing on the moon weighs much less than he or she does on Earth. For example, an astronaut who weights 180 pounds on Earth will weigh only about 30 pounds on the moon. Obviously, the astronaut has not lost 150 pounds on the way to the moon. Rather, the reason the astronaut weighs much less on the moon is because of gravity.

Gravity is a force that pulls on an object, such as an astronaut's body. This force creates what we measure as weight. The stronger the force of gravity, the more an object weighs. The force of gravity on Earth is about six times greater than the force of gravity on the moon. Therefore, a person will weigh about six times more on the Earth than on the moon.

No matter how strong its force, gravity always pulls an object in the same direction. For example, if you throw a ball into the air, the ball will fall directly toward Earth. Gravity will pull the ball directly down, unless it hits something or is blown by the wind. You can see this by doing the following experiment.

Experimental Question
Why do objects always fall straight down?

Necessary Materials
- Scissors
- String
- Paper clip
- Tape
- Two books of equal height and thick enough to stand upright
- Sheet of plain white paper
- Pencil

Procedure
1. Cut a 12-inch piece of string.
2. Tie the paper clip to one end of the string.
3. Tie the other end of the string to the middle of the ruler. Tape the string so that the string cannot slide along the ruler.
4. Place the paper on a table and stand a book upright beside each end of the paper.
5. Place the ends of the ruler on the books. The paper clip must hang freely over the paper.
6. Mark the spot on the paper where the paper clip points to.
7. Raise one end of the ruler about 2 inches above the top of the book. Mark the spot on the paper where the paper clip points to.
8. Raise the end of the ruler about 6 inches above the book. Again mark the spot on the paper where the paper clip points to.
9. Repeat steps 7–8, this time raising the ruler at the other end.

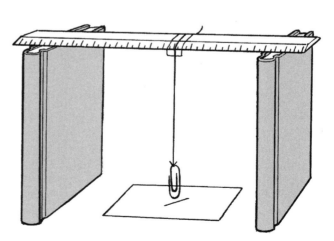

Results and Explanation

The paper clip points to different spots on the paper as you raise the ruler. If you look closely, you will notice that the paper clip always points straight down, no matter how high you raise the ruler at either end. Gravity is a force that always pulls an object toward the center of Earth. Therefore, students performing this experiment anywhere in the world will also find that gravity pulls the paper clip straight down. If the students were on the opposite side of the world, their paper clip would be pointing toward you. In turn, your paper clip would be pointing toward them.

SECONDARY EXPERIMENT

Experimental Question

Does gravity cause heavier objects to fall faster?

Necessary Materials

- Newspaper
- Tall step ladder
- Two apples
- Knife
- Two sheets of plain white paper

Procedure

1. Spread the newspaper on the floor.
2. Place the open ladder in the middle of the newspaper.
3. Ask the adult helper to cut one apple in half.
4. Lie on the floor so that your eyes are almost level with the edge of the newspaper.
5. Ask the adult helper to drop the whole apple and the half apple from the top of the ladder at exactly the same time onto the newspaper.
6. Watch closely to see which one hits the floor first.
7. Next ask the adult to drop the whole apple and grape at the same time.
8. Again watch closely to see if the apple or grape hits the floor first.

9. Tear one sheet of paper in half. Crumple the paper into a small ball.
10. Ask the adult to drop the full sheet of paper and the crumpled half sheet of paper at the same time.
11. Observe which one hits the floor first.

Results and Explanation

The whole apple and the half apple hit the floor at the same time. The whole apple and the grape hit the floor at the same time. However, the crumpled paper hits the floor before the sheet of paper.

The whole apple is heavier than both the half apple and the grape. Many people think that heavier objects fall faster than lighter objects. Yet, the apple, half apple, and grape hit the floor at the same time when they are dropped from the same height. Gravity causes everything to drop to Earth at the same speed, no matter how much it weighs.

However, other forces beside gravity work on objects that fall to Earth. One of these forces is called air resistance. Air resistance can cause a lighter object to fall faster than a heavier object. For example, the crumpled paper falls to the floor faster than the sheet of paper. Yet, the crumpled paper weighs only half as much as the sheet of paper. Although the sheet of paper is heavier, it must push more air out of its way as it falls to the ground. The crumpled paper meets less air resistance on its way down. Therefore, the crumpled paper hits the ground first even though it is lighter than the sheet of paper.

WHAT TIME IS IT?

BACKGROUND INFORMATION

Some clocks, such as a grandfather clock, use a pendulum to keep time. A pendulum is an object called a bob that is attached to a string or wire that swings back and forth. The history of pendulum clocks can be traced to an Italian scientist named Galilei Galileo, who lived from 1564 until 1642.

Galileo was one of the first to carry out experiments to test his ideas. Before his time, most people simply tried to reason why things happen or what would happen. For example, most people believed that a heavier object would always fall faster to the ground. Galileo's experiments showed that this idea was not correct. You discovered this for yourself if you did the Secondary Experiment in "Why Do Objects Fall?"

Galileo also experimented with pendulums. A story tells about Galileo sitting in a church in Pisa, Italy. He noticed that one of the large lamps was swinging back and forth. The lamp was swinging like a pendulum. Galileo noticed that the swing of the lamp was very regular. In other words, the lamp always swung back and forth with the same motion. Galileo wondered what made the lamp swing the way it did. You can find out by doing the following experiment.

Experimental Question

Why is the swing of a pendulum so regular?

Necessary Materials
- Two metal washers
- 12-inch piece of string
- Tape
- Table
- Clock or watch with second hand

Procedure
1. Tie one washer to the end of the string. Tape the other end to an edge of the table. Make sure that the washer can swing freely back and forth like a pendulum.
2. Pull the washer back one foot. Release the washer so that it starts to swing. Count how many times the washer swings back and forth in 30 seconds.
3. Repeat step 2, but this time, pull the washer back 6 inches.
4. Tie another washer to the end of the string.
5. Repeat steps 2 and 3.

Results and Explanation

The number of swings is the same, no matter where the pendulum starts its swing or how heavy the bob. Just as Galileo discovered, you learned that the size of the swing and the weight of the bob do not affect how often a pendulum swings back and forth in the same period of time.

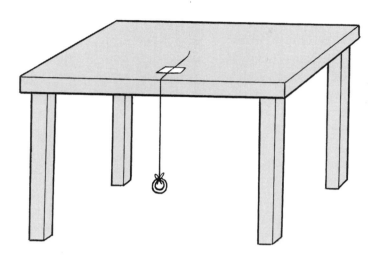

SECONDARY EXPERIMENT

Experimental Question

What can change how a pendulum swings?

Necessary Materials

- Metal washer
- 24-inch piece of string
- Tape
- Table
- Clock or watch with second hand

Procedure

1. Tie the washer to the end of the string. Tape the other end to an edge of the table. Make sure that the washer can swing freely back and forth like a pendulum.
2. Pull the washer back one foot. Release the washer so that it starts to swing. Count how many times the washer swings back and forth in 30 seconds.
3. Compare this number to the number of times the washer swung back and forth when the string was 12 inches long.

Results and Explanation

In the same period of time, the pendulum completes fewer back-and-forth swings when the string is longer. Galileo was the first to discover this fact. He used what he learned about pendulums to design a clock that kept time with a pendulum. Can you adjust the length of the string so that the washer swings back and forth exactly 60 times in one minute? If so, you have a simple pendulum clock that completes one swing every second.

HOW FAST IS THAT CAR GOING?

BACKGROUND INFORMATION

Imagine that you are in a car. Someone asks how fast the car is traveling. You check the speedometer and say 50 miles per hour (mph). This is the car's speed. To determine the speed of an object, you need to know two things. One is the distance. The other is the time. In this example, the car would cover a distance of 50 miles in one hour.

Now suppose someone in the car asks where you are. You suddenly see a road sign saying 95N. You can now tell the person that you are traveling 55 mph heading north on Interstate 95. This is the car's velocity. To determine the velocity of an object, you need to know two things. One is the speed. The other is the direction. In this example, the car's velocity is 50 mph heading north.

Now assume that the car speeds up to 55 miles per hour. Increasing the speed is an example of acceleration. To determine the acceleration of an object, you need to know three things. One is the beginning speed. The second is the final speed. The third is the time. In this example, the car's acceleration is 5 mph because the speed changes from 50 mph to 55 mph. Therefore, the acceleration equals 55 mph (the final speed) minus 50 mph (the beginning speed), or 55 mph - 50 mph = 5 mph.

Experimental Question

How can you determine the speed and velocity of a moving object?

Necessary Materials

- Playground or driveway
- Tape measure
- Colored tape
- Remote-controlled car
- Compass
- Calculator

Procedure

1. Use a tape measure to mark off a distance of 100 feet.
2. Place a piece of tape at both ends to mark this course.
3. Place the car at one end of this course.
4. Have the car travel as fast as possible over this course.
5. Time how long it takes for the car to travel 100 feet.
6. Use the compass to determine the direction the car traveled.
7. Use a calculator to find the speed of the car. Ask an adult if you need help.
8. Determine the car's velocity.
9. Repeat steps 3–5, but this time, make the car travel as slowly as possible.
10. Determine the speed and velocity of the car.

Results and Explanation

Suppose the car takes 50 seconds to travel the 100 feet. Divide the distance (100 feet) by the time (50 seconds). The car's speed is 2 feet per second. If the car were heading in a southwest direction, then the car's velocity is 2 feet per second heading southwest.

The car not only has speed and velocity but also acceleration. The car accelerated when you started it. The car also accelerated when you stopped it. In this case, the car underwent a negative acceleration as it slowed to a stop. For example, the car may slow from 2 feet per second to 1 foot per second. Therefore, the acceleration is 1 foot per second minus 2 feet per second or negative 1 foot per second. A negative acceleration means an object is slowing down. Try the Secondary Experiment to learn more about how acceleration works.

SECONDARY EXPERIMENT

Experimental Question
What can affect the acceleration of an object?

Necessary Materials
- String
- Scissors
- Ruler
- Thick rubber band
- Smooth, flat surface such as a wooden floor or table
- Measuring tape

Procedure
1. Tie a piece of string around a book. Cut the string to leave a piece about 6 inches long.
2. Tie the piece of string through the loop of the rubber band.
3. Place the book on a smooth, flat surface.
4. Ask your helper to pull on the rubber band until the book starts to move.
5. Measure how long the rubber band stretches to get the book moving.
6. Repeat steps 3–4, but this time, place another book on top of the first book.
7. Repeat steps 3–4, but this time, place two books on top of the first book.

Results and Explanation
A force must be applied to get an object to accelerate. Pulling on the rubber band supplies the force to accelerate the book. More force must be applied to accelerate two books. Two books have more mass than one book. Mass is the amount of stuff that makes up an object. The more mass there is, the more force must be applied to accelerate the object. This is why the rubber band stretches more when two books are pulled. Even more force must be applied to accelerate three books. In this case, the rubber band stretches the most. Because a truck has more mass than a car, more force is required to accelerate a truck.

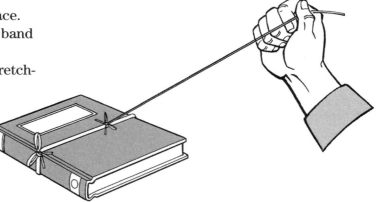

WHY DO SOME THINGS FLOAT?

BACKGROUND INFORMATION

For ages people have known that some objects float while other objects sink. However, for a long time no one knew why. The mystery was finally solved by Archimedes, who was born in Sicily in 287 BCE.

Archimedes' first love was mathematics. He used mathematics to explain what he saw, including why objects float. There is a legend that Archimedes discovered the answer while taking a bath. What Archimedes discovered is known as buoyancy.

An object in water is pulled downward by the force of gravity. However, there is another force pushing upward on the object. The force pushing upward is buoyancy. If the force of gravity is greater than the force of buoyancy, then the object will sink. If the force of buoyancy is greater than the force of gravity, then the object will float. You can change how these forces work so that an object that normally sinks can be made to float.

Experimental Question

How can you get a rock to float?

Necessary Materials

- Towel (optional)
- Large plastic bucket
- Rocks of different sizes
- Large empty jar with tight-fitting lid

Procedure

1. If you are working indoors, spread a towel on the floor.
2. Fill the bucket almost to the top with water.
3. Gently put the rocks, one at a time, into the water.
4. Place the empty jar with the lid closed tightly into the water.
5. Observe what happens to the rocks and jar in the water.
6. Remove the jar and rocks from the water.
7. Open the jar, place the smallest rock inside, and close the lid tightly.
8. Place the jar with the rock in the water.
9. If the jar and rock float, place another rock inside the jar.
10. Close the lid tightly and again place the jar in the water.
11. Repeat steps 9–10 until the jar sinks.

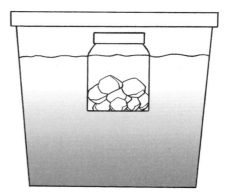

Results and Explanation

The rocks sink, while the empty jar floats. The jar still floats even though you place rocks inside. Eventually, however, the jar will sink when enough rocks have been added. When placed in water, a rock pushes aside some water. This is called displacement. Even the smallest rock displaces some water.

However, the weight of even the smallest rock is greater than the weight of water the rock displaces. If an object weighs more than the water it displaces, then the object will sink.

When placed in water, the jar, which is filled with air, also displaces water. In this case, the jar, lid, and air inside weigh less than the water they displace. As a result, they float. As you add more rocks, the jar gets heavier. As soon as the rocks and jar weigh more than the water they displace, the jar sinks.

Ships float for the same reason. A ball of steel sinks because it weighs more than the water it displaces. However, the same amount of steel can be shaped to form a hollow hull. In this case, the hull, which is filled with air, weighs less than the water it displaces. As a result, the ship floats.

SECONDARY EXPERIMENT

Experimental Question
How can an insect walk on water?

Necessary Materials
- Large bowl
- Fork
- Box of small paper clips
- Liquid detergent
- Spoon

Procedure
1. Fill the bowl with water.
2. Use the fork to gently lower a paper clip onto the water.
3. Use the fork to gently lower another paper clip onto the water.
4. See how many paper clips you can get to float on the water.
5. Remove the paper clips from the water.
6. Add several drops of the liquid detergent to the water.
7. Gently stir the water and detergent to avoid making suds.
8. Repeat steps 2–4.

Results and Explanation
The paper clips float because there is something unusual about water. Water molecules stick to one another. Water molecules stick so closely that they form a thin layer like a skin on the water's surface. The paper clips are too light to break this skin. So, the paper clips float. Many insects are also too light to break this skin. Therefore, these insects can walk on water.

The detergent makes it harder for the water molecules to stick together. As a result, the skin on the water's surface is much easier to break. Therefore, you cannot get as many paper clips to float when you add detergent to the water.

WHY DO COMPASSES POINT NORTH?

BACKGROUND INFORMATION

A magnet is an object that can attract certain metals. Some metals, such as iron and silver, are attracted to a magnet. Other metals, such as gold and aluminum, are not. Magnets come in various sizes and shapes. Large magnets are used to lift scrap metal in junk yards. Small magnets are used to hold pictures on a refrigerator door.

Small magnets are also used in compasses. The reason that compasses work is that Earth itself can be considered a giant magnet. The center of Earth is called its core. The core is filled with melted iron. This melted iron causes Earth to act like a magnet.

Every magnet has two poles. One pole is called its north pole. The other pole is called its south pole. As a giant magnet, Earth has two poles as well: the North Pole and the South Pole. One end of a compass needle points toward the North Pole, and the other end points toward the South Pole.

Experimental Question

Which part of a magnet attracts the best?

Necessary Materials

• Box of paper clips
• Bar magnet

Procedure

1. Open a paper clip to form a hook.
2. Stick the paper clip to one end, either the north pole or south pole, of the magnet.
3. Gently place another paper clip on the hook.
4. Continue adding paper clips to see how many clips the hook can hold.
5. Repeat steps 2–4, but this time, place the hook at the other pole.
6. Repeat steps 2–4, but this time, place the hook in the middle of the magnet.

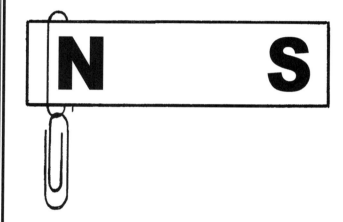

Results and Explanation

The hook can hold more paper clips when it is placed at either pole. The poles of a magnet have the strongest attraction for metal objects. This is why the hook cannot hold as many paper clips when it is placed in the middle of the magnet.

If you suspend the bar magnet from a string, it will act like a compass. One pole will point north. The other pole will point south. The pole that points north is the north-seeking pole, which is simply called the magnet's north pole. The pole that points south is the south-seeking pole, which is simply called its south pole. The bar magnet will act this way no matter where you are on Earth.

SECONDARY EXPERIMENT

Experimental Question
What will happen if the same poles of magnets come close to one another?

Necessary Materials
- Adult helper
- Drill
- Wooden board
- 12-inch wooden dowel
- Wood glue
- Four ceramic ring magnets

Procedure
1. Ask an adult to make a hole in the wooden board to hold the dowel upright. The dowel must be small enough so that it fits through the hole in the magnets.
2. Glue the dowel into the board. Allow the glue to dry.
3. Place one of the ring magnets over the dowel. Lower the magnet so that it rests on the board.
4. Place another ring magnet over the first one. If the two magnets are attracted to each other, remove the second magnet. Flip the second magnet over and again place it over the first magnet.
5. Continue placing the magnets over the dowel. As you place each magnet, make sure that the magnet is not attracted to the one beneath it.
6. Describe what you see.

Results and Explanation
Each magnet should float above the one beneath it. If the same two poles of two magnets are brought together, they will push one another apart. However, the dowel keeps the two magnets in place so that one magnet floats above the other.

Large magnets that are lined up in this way can lift heavy objects. For example, magnets are used to lift trains above the tracks so that they can move without friction from the rails. As a result, these trains can move at very high speeds.

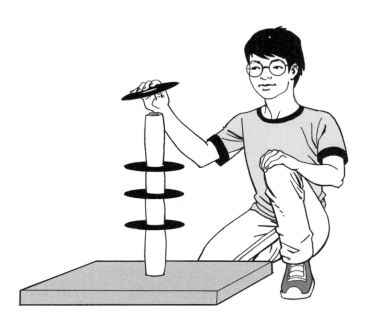

HOW CAN WORK GET EASIER?

BACKGROUND INFORMATION

A simple machine is a device that makes work easier. There are six types of simple machines: the plane, the pulley, the screw, the wedge, the lever, and the wheel and axle. You may have used one of these simple machines at home. For example, you may have used a pencil sharpener, which is an example of a wheel and axle. Or you may have pried something open with the point of a screwdriver, which is an example of a wedge. Now you can find out how much easier it is to lift objects with the help of another simple machine, the lever.

plane   pulley   screw

wedge   lever   wheel & axle

Experimental Question
How does a lever work?

Necessary Materials
- Six books
- Two unsharpened pencils

Procedure
1. Place your index finger under the edge of one book.
2. Try to lift the book with your finger.
3. Place a second book on top of the first one.
4. Try to lift both books with your finger.
5. See how many books you can lift with just your finger.
6. Place one pencil on the floor or table parallel to the spine of one book.
7. Place one end of the second pencil at a right angle and on top of the first pencil. Slip the second pencil under the book.
8. Use your index finger to push down on the second pencil.
9. See how many books you can lift with the help of the two pencils.

Results and Explanation
Using the two pencils allows you to lift more books. The two pencils act as a lever. A lever is made of two parts. One part of a lever moves, while the other part of a lever does not move. The part of a lever that moves is called the lever arm. The pencil you push with your finger is the lever arm. The part of a lever that does not move is called the fulcrum. The fulcrum is the point around which the lever arm moves. The pencil running along the spine of the bottom book is the fulcrum.

SECONDARY EXPERIMENT

Experimental Question
How much can you lift with a lever?

Necessary Materials
• Long, thick wooden plank
• Brick

Procedure
1. Place the brick under the wooden plank close to one end.
2. Ask the adult to stand on the plank near that end.
3. Stand on the other end of the plank and watch what happens.

Results and Explanation
You should lift the adult by standing on the end of the plank. The plank and brick act as a lever. The plank is the lever arm. The brick is the fulcrum. If you cannot lift the adult by standing on the plank, move the brick closer to the end on which the adult is standing. Moving the fulcrum closer to the object that you want to lift makes the job easier.

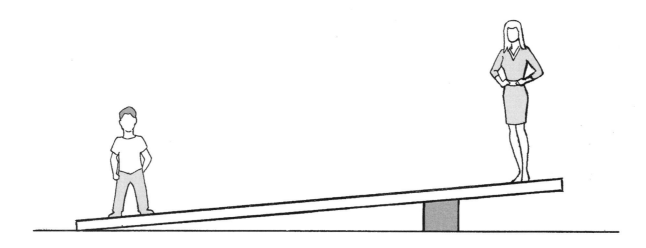

HOW CAN WORK GET EVEN EASIER?

BACKGROUND INFORMATION

Even simple machines may not be enough help to do certain jobs. In this case, you may need the help of a compound machine. A compound machine is made by putting together two or more simple machines. For example, someone may not have the strength to push a heavy carton down an inclined plane. However, the same person would have no trouble pushing the carton down a conveyor. A conveyor is a compound machine that is made from an inclined plane and wheels.

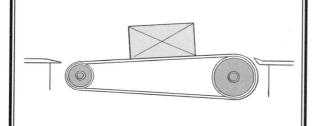

Experimental Question
How does an egg beater work?

Necessary Materials
- Two plastic gears of different sizes
- Two nails that can fit through the center of the gears
- Small cork board
- Colored tape
- Marker

Procedure
1. Use one nail to attach the larger gear to the cork board.

2. Use the second nail to attach the smaller gear to the cork board. Make sure that the teeth of both gears are meshed together. If you turn one gear, the other must turn.
3. Place a tiny piece of colored tape on one tooth of each gear.
4. Use the marker to color two spots on the cork board. One spot should line up with the tooth you marked on the smaller gear. The other spot on the cork board should line up with the tooth you marked on the larger gear.
5. Use your finger to move the larger gear so that it makes one complete turn.
6. Count how many complete turns the smaller gear makes.

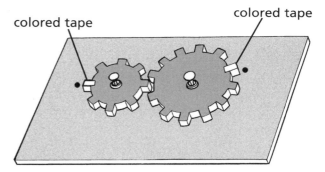

colored tape   colored tape

Results and Explanation
The smaller gear makes more than one complete turn each time the larger gear makes just one complete turn. Overlapping gears of different sizes cause them to turn at different speeds. An egg beater uses gears of different sizes so that the blades spin faster than the handle you turn. An egg beater is an example of a compound machine. Each gear is a wheel. Each blade is a wedge.

Experimental Question

How can you build a compound machine from just one type of simple machine?

Necessary materials

- Two large hooks
- Two pulleys
- Small wooden board
- Clamp
- Table
- Rope
- Scissors
- Large bucket with handle
- Small bucket with handle
- Pennies

Procedure

1. Use a hook to attach the pulley to the board.
2. Clamp the board to the table so that the pulley faces toward the floor.
3. Pass the rope through the pulley.
4. Tie a piece of rope to the large bucket. This bucket should rest on the floor.
5. Tie the other end of the rope to the small bucket. This bucket should be near the pulley.
6. Add the pennies, one at a time, to the smaller bucket, until the larger bucket just lifts off the ground.
7. Count the number of pennies you added to the smaller bucket.

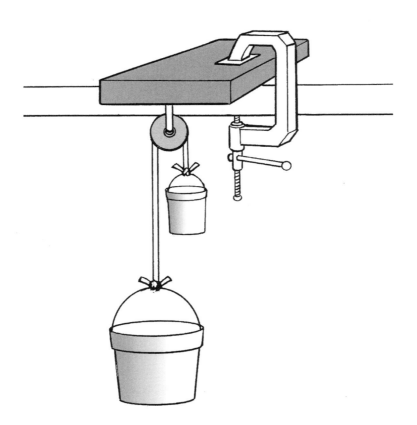

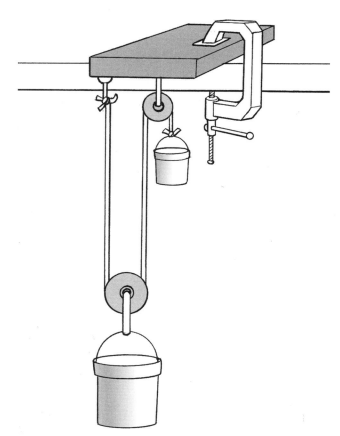

8. Remove the pennies, untie the buckets, and remove the rope from the pulley.
9. Screw in the second hook to the bottom of the board.
10. Tie a piece of rope to the hook.
11. Pass the rope through the second pulley and then through the pulley you attached to the board.
12. Attach the larger bucket to the pulley that is not attached to the board.
13. Tie the smaller bucket to the pulley that is attached to the board.
14. Repeat steps 6–7.

Results and Explanation

When two pulleys are used, fewer pennies are added to the smaller bucket to lift the larger bucket. The two pulleys make up a compound machine. In this case, the compound machine (the two pulleys) makes it easier to lift the large bucket than the simple machine (the one pulley).

Therefore, a compound machine can be made of two identical simple machines. Another example is a scissors, which is a compound machine made from two levers. The two levers make it easy to cut paper.